meet the family
My Dad

by Mary Auld

W
FRANKLIN WATTS
LONDON • SYDNEY

This is Kate with her father. Sometimes she calls him 'Daddy' but mostly just 'Dad'.

Peter's dad was there at Peter's birth. He held his son when he was only a few minutes old.

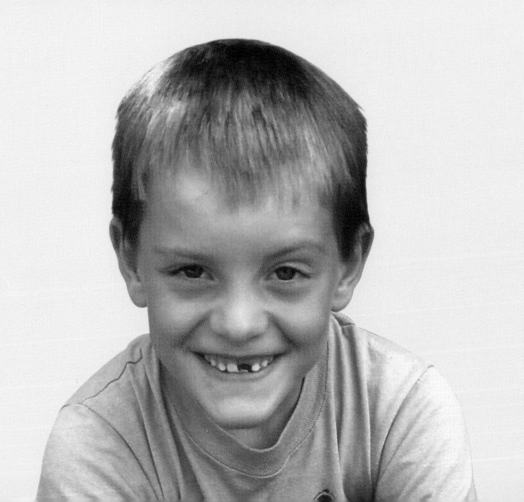

Serena is adopted. Her dad says they became a real family the day Serena arrived.

Claire's step-dad
is called Simon.
He lives with Claire,
her mum and her
baby brother, Kevin.

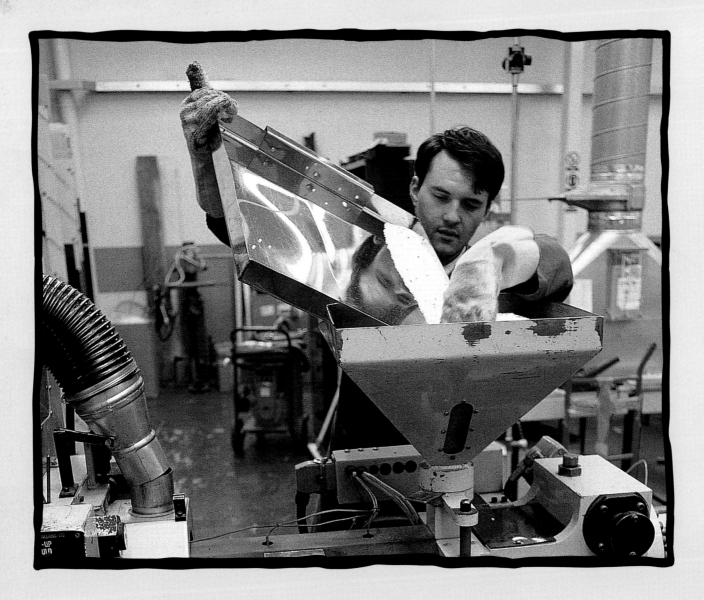

Teresa's dad
works in a factory.

Jackie's dad is a photographer.

Brian's dad is a farmer.

Andy's dad works from home, so he spends a lot of time with Andy, too.

Amanda's dad helps her with her reading after school.

Martin likes helping his dad to cook.

Callum likes going fishing with his dad.

Gurpreet's dad makes sure her safety belt is fastened in the car.

Kevin's dad makes
sure Kevin brushes his
teeth before bedtime.

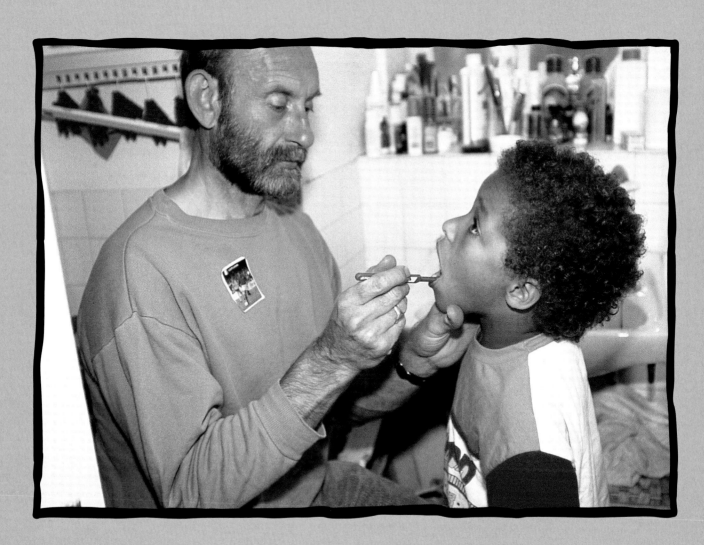

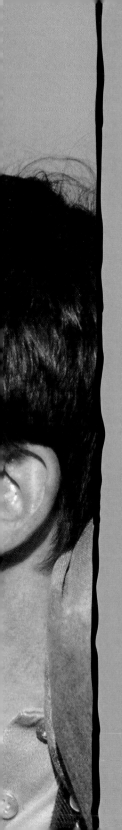

This is Sam, his dad
and his dad's dad –
Grandpa Jim.

What's your dad like?

Family words

Here are some words people use when talking about their dad or family.

Names for dad:
Father, Daddy, Dad, Pa, parent.

Names for mum:
Mother, Mummy, Mum, Ma, parent.

Names of other relatives:
Son, Daughter; Brother, Sister; Grandchildren; Grandparents; Grandmother, Granny, Grandma; Grandfather, Grandad, Grandpa; Uncle; Aunt, Auntie; Nephew, Niece.

If we put the word 'Step' in front of a relative's name it means that we are related to them by marriage but not by birth.

When people are adopted, they become part of a family by law, although they were not born into that family.

A family tree

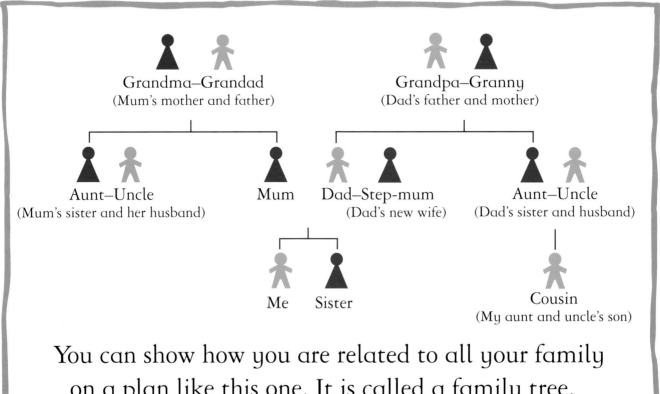

Grandma–Grandad
(Mum's mother and father)

Grandpa–Granny
(Dad's father and mother)

Aunt–Uncle
(Mum's sister and her husband)

Mum

Dad–Step-mum
(Dad's new wife)

Aunt–Uncle
(Dad's sister and husband)

Me   Sister

Cousin
(My aunt and uncle's son)

You can show how you are related to all your family
on a plan like this one. It is called a family tree.
Every family tree is different. Try drawing your own.

First published in 2003 by Franklin Watts,
96 Leonard Street, London EC2A 4XD

Franklin Watts Australia
45-51 Huntley Street, Alexandria, NSW 2015

Copyright © Franklin Watts 2003

Series editor: Rachel Cooke
Art director: Jonathan Hair
Design: Andrew Crowson

A CIP catalogue record for this book
is available from the British Library.

ISBN 0 7496 4884 8

Printed in Hong Kong/China

Acknowledgements:
Bruce Berman/Corbis: front cover centre
below. www.johnbirdsall.co.uk: front cover
centre top, 2, 4, 6, 7, 8, 18. Joanne
O'Brien/Format: 1, 13-14. Carlos
Goldin/Corbis: front cover centre above. Don
Gray/Photofusion: 5. Richard Greenhill, Sally
& Richard Greenhill: 10. Ronnie Kauffman/
Corbis: 20. Roy Morsch/Corbis: 17. Jose Luis

Pelaez/Corbis: front cover main, 22. Ulrike
Press/Format: 11, 19. Chuck Savage/ Corbis:
16. George Shelley/Corbis: front cover bottom.
Ariel Skelley/Corbis: front cover centre, 12.
Christa Stadtler/Photofusion: 13.

Whilst every attempt has been made to clear
copyright should there be any inadvertent
omission please apply in the first instance to
the publisher regarding rectification.